Hot Stuff
to Help Kids
Worry Less:
The
Anxiety Management
Book

Hot Stuff to Help Kids Worry Less:

The Anxiety Management Book

Jerry Wilde, Ph.D.
Jack Wilde

Illustrations by
Anna Wilde

LGR Publishing, Inc.
3219 N. W. C St.
Richmond, IN 47374

LGR Publishing, Inc.
3219 N. W. C St.
Richmond, IN 47374

Hot Stuff to Help Kids Worry Less

For information: LGR Publishing
(800) 369 - 5611

Printing History
First Printing 2008

ISBN-10 : 0-9657610-8-8
ISBN-13: 978-0-9657610-8-6

PRINTED IN THE UNITED STATES OF AMERICA
10 9 8 7 6 5 4 3 2 1

Acknowledgments

There are several people we'd like to thank for helping us with this book. Let's start with wife/mom, Polly Wilde. Not only did she create another great looking cover for the book, she provided a lot of encouragement throughout this little "family project." More importantly, our family would collapse into utter chaos within about 17 hours if it weren't for her. We love you!

The field of psychotherapy lost a true giant on July 24, 2007 with the passing of Dr. Albert Ellis. There is no way I could ever thank Dr. Ellis enough for his assistance both personally and professionally. When I was a young professional, he took the time to correspond with me, which was inspiring. A few years later, he agreed to write an introduction to my first book. The highlight of my career came in 2002 when we co-authored *Case Studies in REBT with Children and Adolescents*. When our daughter was born, the world's most influential (and busiest) therapist took the time to send my wife and me a congratulatory note. Albert Ellis created the system that I have used throughout the *Hot Stuff* books. Without his groundbreaking work, you'd be doing something other than reading this book right now. Thank you, Al. I will do my very best to continue the work you started more than 50 years ago. You are missed.

Last, but certainly not least, this book is dedicated to the memory of Donna Albright, an award winning poet, writer, and teacher. We miss you, Grandma.

A Short Note to the Adults

Welcome! For those of you who have read some of my earlier *Hot Stuff* books, I'd like to extend a very special "thank you" for your continued support. The *Hot Stuff* series started in 1997 on an old Macintosh computer. We're now approaching 100,000 copies in print which absolutely blows my mind. Obviously, there seems to be a need for these books and I'm very grateful to have had the opportunity to introduce these ideas to so many children and families.

On behalf of the children and adolescents, I'd also like to thank you for your interest in the welfare of the next generation. Kids need our help now more than ever because it's much harder growing up today. This generation has so much more to deal with. We have to remain optimistic because what a lot of children and adolescents *really* want is time and attention from a caring adult (like you). In a lot of cases, concerned

1

counselors, educators, and parents are what these kids really need.

I've tried to make this book easily understandable so students can work independently if they chose to do so. There will undoubtedly be times when they will need your assistance because there is only so much a book can accomplish. I like to think of these books as tools designed to introduce ideas and start discussions. However, even the very best tools only create the *possibility* for change. Ultimately, it depends on the skills of the builders. So be patient because the readers will need plenty of reassurance and lots of practice before they are able to add these skills to their own toolboxes. (Yes, I realize I've run the tool metaphor into the ground so let's move on, shall we?)

You'll notice that this book doesn't contain chapters in a traditional sense. Over the years, I've noticed that some adults feel pressured to finish a chapter or adhere to some type of schedule. It's easy to miss "teachable moments" that way. Please don't make

2

that mistake. If a child isn't understanding a certain concept, take the time necessary to clear up the confusion.

I sincerely hope you find this book to be a useful addition to your personal or professional library. If you have any questions or comments feel free to contact me at (765) 939–8924 or info@angerchillout.com. Best of luck and please keep up the important work that you do!

And to the Parents...

After many years spent working with children and families, I can anticipate one question that is usually asked by parents during the course of our time together: **Is this problem our fault?**

I used to try to avoid the question by saying something like, "That's a fair question but it's really not important at this point. Let's focus on the future rather than the past." I wasn't "ducking the question" because I didn't know the answer. I knew that a majority of studies found that there did appear to be a genetic link. Simply put, if your parents were diagnosed with an anxiety disorder, you have a much greater likelihood of suffering from a similar disorder. This is especially true if your parents were diagnosed with panic disorder. However, genetics only explains about 30 to 40% of anxiety disorders so a majority of children with anxious parents never actually develop significant problems related to anxiety. These disorders are best explained through a combination of factors such as genetics, temperament and environmental conditions. However, my explanations changed when I stopped thinking solely as a therapist and started speaking as a father.

I have two children. My daughter, Anna, is 13 and my son, Jack, is ten. My wife and I haven't had any major changes in our beliefs about raising children between their births. Anna and Jack have both been raised in a similar fashion. There haven't been any traumatic events in our lives (knock wood) that would create added stress on our family. Despite being parented in pretty much the same way, they are very, very different. (I know *a lot* of parents are nodding their heads in recognition right about now!) Anna is "Miss Mellow" and never worries about much of anything. In fact, her mother and I would like her to worry a little more about her schoolwork and other responsibilities. Jack, on the other hand, *is* a worrier. In fact, a lot of the ideas in this book have been tried with Jack (and hundreds of other kids). Worries have always had a way of bouncing off Anna but they stick to Jack. Keep in mind they have the same genetic blueprint so the hereditary factor can only explain some of the results some of the time. Was there anything we did to make Jack a worrier and Anna so laid-back? In a word, "nope." That's just part of their personalities; part of the qualities that make them wonderful, weird, and unique. My perspective as a parent helps when I talk to moms and dads of anxious kids.

I also want to point out that the concepts and techniques presented are research-based and field-tested. The model presented in the book is based on cognitive-behavior therapy (CBT), which has extensive empirical evidence verifying its effectiveness in the treatment of anxiety. Various studies find that between 50%-80% of children who receive CBT treatment show significant reduction in their symptoms. What is even more impressive is that these improvements are maintained years later when follow-up studies are conducted. If you are searching for a mental health professional to help your child, I'd recommend that you ask if the therapist has training in CBT. And while this book should not be considered to be a substitute for treatment, I also believe it has the potential to help a lot of children and adolescents.

I'd like to address one more thing before we get to the "meat and potatoes" of the book. I often see parents trying to remove all possible sources of anxiety from

6

their child's life. These efforts are made out of love but ultimately, they are doomed to fail. **Worriers will find things to worry about.** Ultimately, it was my son who helped me learn this lesson. Jack had gone through several common childhood anxieties such worrying about storms or robbers but then there was a period of time where he was anxious about the possibility of throwing up. How could his mother and I guarantee that wouldn't happen? The only way would be to stop feeding him and, obviously, that wasn't an option. With kids who are prone to worry, if you eliminate one anxiety-provoking situation, they'll usually find another one to fret about. Parents can't win this game. So the goal is to teach kids the skills to cope with their worries. In some regards, it is like the old Biblical parable, "If you give a man a fish, he eats today. If you teach him how to fish, he eats tomorrow." If you plan things very carefully, you can probably keep kids' worries to a minimum but you've done nothing to help them overcome their fears. Well, the goal of this book

7

is to teach you and your children how to fish for yourselves. Thanks for taking the time to check out our book.

Introduction

Hello and welcome to "the book." For some reason, you've decided to read this book which could mean several things:

1) You have absolutely nothing to do and you're so bored that you are going completely insane. Reading this book seemed better than taking out the garbage, cleaning your room, or flossing the family cat.

2) At this very moment, an adult is forcing you to read this book. The choice is either to read this book or receive some type of punishment like being grounded or scrubbing the toilet with a toothbrush. After giving it some thought, you chose the book. (Good call!)

3) You were hit in the head during gym class in a game of "bombardment" (also known as dodge ball) and just came to your senses. Ever since getting knocked out, you've been behaving strangely.

4) You want to learn how to control your

worrying.

I hope the answer was # 4 but even if it was numbers 1, 2, or 3, what the heck…just keep on reading.

Before we get going, I thought you might like to know a little about us and why we created this book.

Name:	Jerry Wilde
Job:	Psychologist
Hair:	Got plenty
Wife:	One (Polly)
Favorite Bands:	(old school) AC/DC, Led Zeppelin, Thin Lizzy, UFO (new school) Katatonia, Clutch, Neurosis and hundreds of others
Hobbies:	Listening to music, running, playing guitar, reading books, refusing to be too serious

Cool Things:	music, my family, Green Bay Packers, Iowa Hawkeyes, Minnesota Twins & Diet Mt. Dew
Uncool Things:	Ignorance, wasting time, judgmental people and meetings

Name:	Jack Wilde
Primary Job:	Student, 4th grader
Secondary Job:	To annoy my sister
Cats:	One (Spazmo...R.I.P. Moshie and Herb)
Dogs:	Two, Theo (the fat brown one) and Roscoe (the black obnoxious one)
Hobbies:	Guitar Hero, baseball, basketball, playing Runescape online (account jackwilde), video games

Favorite Movies:	The Rookie, Freaky Friday, Sandlot (except for the puking scene…gross!)
Cool Things:	Root Beer, friends, pizza, McDonalds
Uncool Things:	Big sisters, waking up early, homework, shrimp, fried onions

Name:	Anna Wilde
Primary Job:	Student, 7th grader
Secondary Job:	the book's illustrator and to pound on my bother
Cats and Dogs:	see above
Hobbies:	listening to music, hanging out with friends, softball, band (French horn), piano
Favorite Movies:	Dodgeball, Napoleon Dynamite, The Simpsons, The Fox and the Hound

Cool Things:	Hawkeyes, music, my pets, my best friends, band
Uncool Things:	doing homework, doing chores, my bro, green beans, mustard, not being able to drive

We decided to work on this book because we think we can help you learn the skills necessary to understand and overcome feelings of anxiety and worry. I (Jerry) have written several other books about anxiety, but they were for counselors and psychologists, not for students. This one is just for you.

It dawned on me that it would be a good idea to get a kid's perspective so I asked Jack to help me out. He agreed to be my co-author because he knew I'd ground him if he said no. Just kidding. Jack thought it was a good idea because he's had difficulties with worrying, too. I told him the book would include a lot of the stuff we worked on to help him get better at handling his worries.

We're ready to get started except for one thing…the hard part. Are you ready to hear about the hard part? You had to know there had to be a catch, didn't you? There's always a catch. Okay, here it is.

Since there really isn't any magic in the world, **you won't feel differently if you don't think and act differently.** Your friends, parents, teachers, dogs, cats, and gerbils can't *make* you feel better. We certainly can't magically fix your life with a book, but we can help you learn some ideas and activities that have been proven to work. To feel better you're going to have to actually *do* some of the things that will be suggested in this book. Your life won't suddenly be perfect, but you'll have the opportunity to learn some skills that will put you in charge of your feelings.

Over the years, I have worked with hundreds of students and they've had a lot of luck with the ideas I'm going to teach you. You can learn to have a happier life, but it will not be easy. If you work hard at the things in this book, you'll probably feel better. If you don't work hard, you probably won't feel any differently. **The choice is totally up to you.** But keep in mind, you are also free to experience all the worries and unhappiness your heart can bear.

Learning to control your anxieties is like learning any new skill. It takes a lot of hard work and practice. There are absolutely no shortcuts, but the rewards are worth the effort.

The first half of the book will be explaining important concepts about worrying and anxiety. The last half will be spent applying what you've learned to your life. Now, it's time to get to work.

Anxiety in America

We live in scary times. Have you turned on the news lately? War, terrorists, mad cow disease, bird flu, and kids being abducted seem to be happening all the time. It should come as no surprise that anxiety disorders are the most common form of mental health problem in America. Over 15 million adults suffer from anxiety disorders each year. You know what's weird? Out of those 15 million, less than 30% actually seek treatment. I think that's weird because if I broke my arm, I'd go the hospital. I wouldn't just keep a stiff upper lip and hope my arm stopped hurting. What I'm saying is there's nothing cool about suffering in silence. That's not being brave and tough. The really brave people step up and say, "I've got a problem and I need help." That takes a heck of a lot more courage than just quietly suffering on your own. So, even though I don't know you personally, I'm proud of you for deciding to get help with what's bugging you because you've taken a huge step toward learning to manage your worries.

The 15 million people mentioned above are all adults. How are kids doing with anxiety? Well, between 5 and 15% of all children suffer from some type of anxiety disorder making it the most common psychological condition facing children today. So, you are not alone. It is also common for kids who have difficulties with anxiety to struggle with other problems like depression. Girls tend to have a greater chance of being diagnosed with an anxiety disorder. Sometimes it may feel like you're alone but there are thousands of children and adolescents struggling with the same problems.

What is Anxiety?

There are a lot of different names for anxiety. Some people call it being "scared" or "stressed out." Others simply call it "worrying." I've also heard people call it "nervousness" or being "uptight." Whatever you want to call it, anxiety is basically the way your body reacts to a certain type of thought. Yes, you read that right. **Anxiety is a feeling but it is created by a thought.** We'll get back to that idea a little later but right now I want to clarify something before we go any further.

Worrying isn't necessarily a bad thing and the goal of this book is not to try to stop you from ever worrying again. Worrying can be a good thing because it helps protect us. It's a type of defense system to keep us out of dangerous situations.

If you were standing in line waiting for lunch and all of a sudden, you heard a very loud "**BANG**," your

18

body would react because it would identify the sound as a potential threat. You'd go through changes to get ready to either "fight or flight." Your body would immediately start producing something called *adrenaline,* which would make you ready for quick action. Your heart would pump blood to your arms and legs to make you better able to defend yourself (fight) or get away (flight). These reactions have been around for a millions of years and they help keep us safe.

So the goal is not to be "fear-less." That would be stupid. If you were at the zoo looking at a den of lions, it wouldn't be wise to be "fear-less" and say to yourself, "I'm going to climb in there with those lions. They look friendly." Your brain would flash the message: **Warning! Warning! Are you out of your mind? This is dangerous!** If you were doing tricks on your bike and a friend challenged you to jump a ramp while blindfolded, it would only make sense to feel anxious about the possibility of getting hurt. In fact, I'll bet you can name someone you know who does dangerous things without ever giving it a second thought. It seems like every school has a daredevil (or two) who could use a little more fear! It might keep them out of the emergency room.

On the lines below write down your own example of how anxiety can help protect us from doing dumb and/or dangerous things:

_____

_____

_____

_____

_____

_____

But sometimes our worry muscle (i.e., the brain) can work *too* well. It can cause us to worry about something that is probably never going to happen or if it did, it wouldn't be that big a deal. Have you ever heard of the expression "making a mountain out of a molehill?" That's what an anxious brain can do. You start thinking about something that will probably never happen and then it gets stuck in your brain. My guess is you are one of those kids. You worry about too many things…things that probably won't happen AND you worry for too long. You don't seem to be able to stop yourself from worrying. Those thoughts are like glue that get stuck in your brain.

People say, "Don't worry so much," but that doesn't help. Your parents say, "Just forget about it," but that doesn't help either. If you could stop worrying on your own, you would. Well, that's where this book comes in. It's designed to help you get unstuck. These pages are going to teach you things that will help you learn to control your anxiety.

But right now let's take a closer look at the kinds of attitudes you have. Your thoughts and attitudes about things are extremely important in the type of skills you are going to be learning. Take a minute and complete the survey below. There are no right or wrong answers, just circle the number which best reflects how strongly you agree or disagree with each statement. You're also going to do this survey at the end of the book to see what kind of progress you've made.

The Anxiety Survey

Strongly   Strongly
Disagree   Agree

1. If something bad might happen, I have to worry about it.

     1   2   3   4   5   6

2. I have no control over my worrying.

     1   2   3   4   5   6

3. Worrying about something can keep it from happening.

  1   2   3   4   5   6

4. If what I worry about *did* happen, it would be the worst thing in the world.

  1   2   3   4   5   6

5. My worries have a "mind of their own" and can't be managed.

  1   2   3   4   5   6

6. If what I worry about *did* happen, I couldn't stand it.

  1   2   3   4   5   6

7. Because I worry about things, it proves I'm worthless and weak.

  1   2   3   4   5   6

8. Worries never seem to go away. Once you've got them, you're stuck with them.

  1   2   3   4   5   6

TOTAL_____

The Top 5 Ways Your Worries are Messing Up Your Life

Chances are you already realize that anxiety is causing problems in your life...otherwise, why would you be reading this book? There are many ways worrying too much can mess up your life and we're going to look at some of the big ones.

1. Embarrassment

Answer the following questions.

Have you ever been embarrassed by something you've done because of your worries? **Yes   No**
It's okay to be honest. You are not alone here.

Have you ever had to come up with an excuse to cover up for the fact that you're worried about something? **Yes   No**

Have you ever embarrassed your family or friends with your worries? **Yes   No**

Take a few minutes and write down something embarrassing you've done because of your worries.

_____

_____

_____

_____

_____

_____

2. Missing Out on the "Good Stuff" in Life

Your worries can cause you to miss out on a lot of fun stuff. Your worries hold you back like a heavy stone tied around your neck. For example, have you had to miss out on a sleepover because you were too worried about being away from your home or your parents? That's just one example. There are thousands of others.

Have you ever missed out on something that would have been fun because of your worries? **Yes No** If you answered "yes," describe it below.

_____

_____

_____

_____

_____

_____

_____

3. Wasted Time and Energy

Think about this for a minute, what has your anxiety ever gotten for you?

Has your anxiety made you any friends? **Yes   No**

Has anyone ever paid you to worry?   **Yes No**

Has worrying ever helped you meet a girl/guy?

Yes No

Has anyone ever told you, "I think you're really cool because you worry a lot"?   **Yes No**

26

Has anyone ever given you free pizza because you get anxious easily?   **Yes No**

What has your anxiety ever gotten you other than into trouble?

That's why anxiety is usually a waste of time and energy. It rarely accomplishes anything positive. It does take a lot of work to worry. It wastes the energy you need to live.

Here's something else to think about. Not only is worrying usually a waste of time, it doesn't prevent bad things from happening. Jack used to be worried about getting hit by a baseball when he was at bat. Do you think that worry is going to keep the ball from hitting him? Will it provide a "force field" of protection for him? Nope. Eventually he got "plunked" and then he said, "Oh, that wasn't too bad. It hurt a bit but only for a minute." All that worrying did nothing to help him and it made it harder for him to concentrate when he was hitting. He also used to worry about storms but did his worrying change the weather? It sure didn't.

4. Friendship Problems

Anxiety also has a way of causing problems with your friendships. If you're like most people with anxiety problems, you have to change your life to cope with your worries. That means you have to miss going over to a friend's house because they might have a dog or because it might thunder and lightening while you're there. You don't want to admit that you're scared to your friend so you make up an excuse. "I can't come over today…I'm busy." Eventually your friend might misunderstand and think, "Maybe it's because she (or he) doesn't want to be my friend." That's a real shame because friendships are one of the best parts of life.

5. Your Health

When people worry, their bodies are always in a state of "high alert." Even when things are going just fine, their minds wander to thoughts like, "If I go over to Ben's house, I wonder if his basement has spiders" or "I hope my parents don't forget to sign that permission form for the field trip tomorrow." People who have anxiety problems are always looking for the next potential threat or problem.

Having to stay mentally "keyed-up" can be hard on your health. You may get headaches or stomachaches. Some kids chew their fingernails to the nub or they might catch more colds and flu because their immune system is run down from all the energy they spend worrying. On the spaces below, write down the places you "feel" the anxiety in your body.

1. _____

2. _____

3. _____

Now, take out a blank piece of paper and draw a picture of what your anxiety feels like. It doesn't matter if you're not the world's greatest artist. There seems to be something healthy about getting those images put down on paper. It puts you in control.

So What Causes You To Get Anxious Anyway?

That is the million-dollar question. What causes your anxiety?

Is it your parents?

Is it your brothers and sisters?

Is it your teachers?

Is it your friends?

Is it your dog or cat?

Is it a rainy day?

Is it the full moon?

Is it a bad hair day?

Is it the price of CDs and video games?

The answer to all these questions is **no!**

No matter what you think, none of the things mentioned above can **make** you anxious. You, and only you, control your feelings. So the answer to the million dollar question is three little letters. What makes you anxious?

Y - O - U

I can hear some of you saying, "The Wilde boys have definitely gone off the deep end. They don't have both oars in the water. The lights are on but nobody's home. They're crazy if they think *I* make myself worry too much. I hate it. Why would I do that to myself?"

If you don't believe us, let's see if we can prove it to you with a story. Let's pretend you were walking down the hall at school and somebody came up behind you and knocked all your books out of your hands. How would you feel? You'd start whistling a happy tune, right? No, seriously, how would you feel? If you're like most people, you'd probably be angry or anxious or maybe both.

But when you turned around to see who hit your books, you realized it was a blind student who

31

accidentally bumped into you. He couldn't see where he was going and he bumped into you. *Now* how would you feel? Would you still feel angry and/or anxious? Probably not.

Here's the important part. You still got your books knocked out of your hands so **this event** (having your books scattered) can't make you feel anything. People would have different reactions to having their books knocked around. Some would feel angry, some would get anxious, and others would laugh it off along with everyone else. **If events caused feelings, then everyone would feel the same way after the same events**. But people don't feel the same way about things. People tend to feel differently about events so the experiences don't cause emotions. It must be something else.

That "something else" is your **thoughts**. Your thoughts, beliefs, and ideas determine your feelings…not the events. Let's take a closer look at the example of getting your books knocked out of your hands. This is crucial to the rest of the ideas in the book so let's make certain it's perfectly clear.

What would you probably be **thinking** just after your books went flying?

_____

_____

_____

_____

It might be something like, "Oh, no. Somebody is trying to hurt me or make me look stupid." Those thoughts would make most people anxious.

Now, what would you **think** to yourself when you saw it was a blind student?

_____

_____

_____

_____

Maybe something like, "He didn't mean to do it. It was an accident." Those thoughts would probably calm you down.

Notice how the event (getting your books scattered) stayed the same but the feelings changed when your thoughts changed. That's because **your thoughts influence (and largely control) your feelings.**

This is great news. If other people and things made you anxious, what would be the point of trying to learn to handle your worries? There wouldn't be a point because you would have no control. Other people and events would be controlling you like a puppet.

Plus, if events made you anxious, then everybody would be anxious about the same things. And we're not, are we? Things that worry some people (like thunderstorms or being home alone) don't bother you at all and the things you worry about don't bother most other people so it can't be "things" that make you anxious.

Now that we've answered the million-dollar question, we have our work cut out for us. Next, we need to learn how to start hearing those thoughts before getting anxious. It's not easy, but with some practice you'll get the hang of it.

Some of you still might be wondering about the connections between thoughts and feelings. That's cool. I don't think it's wise to believe anything just because somebody told you it was so. Jack and I will try to convince you that thoughts and feelings are connected by giving you some *proof.* As we'll learn later, it's usually a good idea to look for proof.

Below is a list of thoughts. Your job is to match the feeling that would go with each thought. You'll probably be able to do this pretty easily. Why? Because thoughts influence feelings. If they didn't, your answers would be totally different from your friends but I'll bet they'll be mostly the same. Give this a try and see how it goes.

Thoughts and Feelings

What type of feeling would you have if you thought:

"Oh, no...I didn't know there was a test today."

Feeling_____

"What do you mean I'm grounded?"

Feeling_____

"I'm worthless. Everyone hates me."

Feeling_____

"Life stinks."

Feeling_____

"I hope my parents won't forget to pick me up after basketball practice."

Feeling_____

"It's snowing hard right now. We might have a day off of school tomorrow."

Feeling_____

"My mom and dad are having an argument."

Feeling_____

See, that wasn't hard to do, was it? Now that you're starting to understand the connection between thoughts and feelings, let's move on. It's time to start focusing in on *your* worries.

Below is a list of things that some kids worry about. Next to each item, check either "yes, I worry about it" or "no, I don't worry about it." If you checked yes, there's another column where you can record your rating from 1 to 100. This rating is called a SUDs scale, which stands for "Subjective Units of Discomfort." Scores closer to 1 mean you have less worries and scores nearer to 100 mean you have more worries. Your lowest score should be the item you have the least worries about and your highest score would be the event that you worry about the most.

My Worry List

	Yes	No	SUDs Score
Ghosts/Monsters	____	____	____
Thunderstorms	____	____	____
Spiders or other bugs	____	____	____
Being away from my parents	____	____	____
Doctors/Dentists	____	____	____
Being made fun of	____	____	____
Feeling left out by my friends	____	____	____
Getting hurt	____	____	____
A terrorist attack	____	____	____
Something happening to my parents	____	____	____
Tests at school	____	____	____
Doing poorly at school	____	____	____

	Yes	No	SUDs Score
Shots/Injections	___	___	___
Snakes	___	___	___
Feeling Pain	___	___	___
Fires	___	___	___
Burglars/robbers	___	___	___
Getting in trouble	___	___	___
The dark	___	___	___
Elevators	___	___	___
Escalators	___	___	___
Choking	___	___	___

How Worries Get Started

As we explained a little bit earlier, worries (and all other feelings) come from thoughts. But worries don't come from just any thought. If you had the thought, "I love ice cream," you wouldn't feel anxious. Worries come from certain types of thoughts that are usually related to the possibility of something bad happening. Look over your "My Worries" list. Each item on the list *could* lead to something bad happening. For example, some kids are afraid of dogs because dogs *could* bite them. Others are afraid of being away from their parents because they're worried something *might* happen to their moms and dads. So most worries have at least one thing in common. There is the potential for something bad happening.

But think about this, is there *any* event that doesn't at least have the possibility of something bad happening? Wouldn't it be possible to win the lottery and then get a really bad paper cut from the check? Couldn't you get the bike you've always wanted and then wipe out? If your parents would let you eat all the ice cream in the world, you could get a severe case of "brain freeze."

So where do worries really come from? They come from exaggerating the "badness" of the bad outcome. I know that's not the correct way to say it but it seems to make sense to the kids I've worked with over the years. It's making the badness even badder! It's taking a bad event making it ten times worse by letting your imagination run away with you. Here's an example that might make this easier to understand.

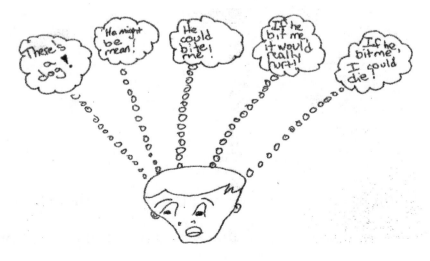

Sure, a dog could bite you but there are many things worse than being bitten by a dog. I'll list three things I think are worse than getting chomped by a dog.

1. Having your foot run over by a pick-up truck.
2. Having to wear a pair of underwear on the outside of your clothes everyday for the rest of your life.
3. Having to eat spinach three times a day for the rest of your life.

Those are my three, now it's your turn to list your three. What are three things worse than being bitten by a dog?

1. _____

   _____

2. _____

   _____

3. _____

   _____

Now it's time to apply this idea to your worries. If you have a # 1 worry, write it down here. Think of a # 1 worry as the thing that you worry the most about.

My # 1 worry is:

_____

_____

_____

_____

Okay, time for the same drill. What are three things *worse* than your # 1 worry?

1. _____

_____

2. _____

_____

3. _____

_____

    The point of this exercise is to try to help you gain some perspective. Sometimes we get ourselves so worked up worrying about the possibility of a bad event that *worrying* about it is worse than when it actually happens! For me (Jerry), that used to be true when I worried about trips to the dentist. Then we'd go and it was never that bad. The worry was worse than the event. Have you ever been really worried about an upcoming event and when it happened, it was no big deal? If so, write it down below.

_____

_____

_____

_____

_____

But for some of you, your # 1 worry is something that would change your life forever like something bad happening to a parent or maybe a terrorist attack or a natural disaster. You probably won't be able to list three things worse than your # 1 (but try anyway). If this is you, your worries are coming from an entirely different place. **Your worries are coming from exaggerating the possibility of the bad event really happening.**

44

Let's say your worries are related to another terrorist attack like the one that took place on 9/11. While a terrorist attack is always possible, the odds of you personally being harmed are incredibly slim. That's because your brain gets stuck on a certain worries and completely ignores other potential dangers. For example, I'll bet you didn't know that there have been more than 50 people killed by falling vending machines since 1978. Yet, I've never met a single person who constantly worries about being crushed to death by a pop machine.

That's sort of like people who are afraid to fly on planes. They know that they are much safer traveling by plane than by car but they are still worried. And you know why? Knowing something in your brain is much different than feeling it in your "gut." When your brain and your "gut" get into a disagreement, your "gut" usually wins. At least for a few rounds until the brains gets better prepared.

This last section may have helped some of you

quite a bit. It was intended to give you a different way to think about your worries. These new ideas might give you a better understanding of how "you" create and can control your worries. But some readers haven't been helped by this section one little bit. That's because this last section was appealing to your logical brain. When your worries kick in, your logical brain says, "bye, bye." I understand that completely. Some people need a different approach and that's fine. Think of this book as an "all you can eat" restaurant. I'm going to present a lot of different ideas. Your job is to look them over (like the food in the buffet line), and pick the ones that sound (or look) good to you. If some of these ideas don't interest you (like brown lettuce or funky looking cottage cheese), just pass right by and look for something better (hello chocolate pudding!).

Distraction

Of course the goal of all this is to help you learn how **not** to make yourself anxious when you are faced with a difficult situation. There are things you can do while you're learning these skills to keep yourself out of trouble. One of the best is a technique called distraction.

It's actually pretty simple. Distraction requires you to force yourself to think of something other than the situation you're getting anxious about. But you know what happens? When you're getting anxious the **only** thing you seem to be able to think about is the situation that you're worrying about. It's like there's a little hammer inside your head knock, knock, knocking on your brain. That's why you need to decide what you're going to think about to distract yourself **before** you start getting anxious.

So, the first step is to pick a memory to think

about prior to that situation. This memory should be either the happiest or funniest thing you can remember. For example:

-The time you hit a home run to win a game.

-The time you got the perfect present for Christmas.

-Your best birthday party ever.

-The time you said something funny and your friends laughed so hard that milk came out of their noses.

-The time you had an unexpected day off from school because of a snow storm.

I use a scene from a few years ago when our cat Spazmo tried to steal a hot dog off the kitchen table. At the time, Spazmo was a little kitten and the hot dog was about half as big as she was. Spazmo was dragging it across the floor like it was a tree. Every time I imagine Spazmo doing battle with that hot dog, I crack up laughing. There is no way I could be anxious or worried when I'm thinking about that scene.

Take a few minutes and think about your distraction scene and then write it down below. This is important so think of a good scene.

Now you need to **practice** imagining this scene several times daily for the next few days. When you're sitting on the bus or waiting in line to eat lunch, just close your eyes and picture your distraction scene as clearly as you can. Bring in all the details that you can possibly remember.

What were the people wearing?

What were the sounds around you?

Were there any smells in the air?

Try to make the scene in your mind just like watching a video.

The plan is to switch to this scene when you find yourself getting anxious. Instead of thinking about your # 1 worry, concentrate on your scene. Whenever you feel yourself getting anxious, switch to your distraction scene.

There is no way you can think of your distraction scene and still become anxious. It's impossible. Since anxiety is produced by thoughts, thinking about a funny or happy memory will keep you from getting upset. It will give you time to relax and chill. That few seconds of time could be the difference between handling a situation and letting the "worry monster" take over.

My Very Best "Trick"

Now it's time to actually practice using your distraction scene. Most kids who worry too much usually have one or two situations that give them trouble. They always worry about the same stuff. If that is true for you, I have something great to teach you. This is my very best trick so use it with care. If this power were to fall into the wrong hands, there's no telling what would happen! The world could be brought to its knees!! Just kidding, but it is pretty cool and it has helped a lot of people.

The technique is called rational-emotive imagery and it is fairly easy to do. First you have to imagine a situation where you get anxious. It can be your # 1 worry if you want it to be but it's okay to start with something other than that. Close your eyes and imagine the situation clearly. Pretend you are actually there in your mind. See all the things going on in that situation.

Hear the sounds that would be around you and everything about the scene. Make it as real as possible. On a scale of 1-100, how anxious were you when this event happened in real life? Score _____

Next, imagine the scene like it is when you worry too much. Go ahead and let yourself feel anxious just like you would if it were real life. Let yourself feel anxious for 15 - 30 seconds. On a scale of 1-100, how anxious were you when you imagined the scene in your mind? Score _____

Now, instead of being really, really anxious, **calm yourself down**. Stay in that scene in your mind but keep working until you get yourself calmed down. Do whatever you need to do to calm yourself. When you get to the point where you've gotten your anxiety under control, take a deep breath and open up your eyes. Below, write down exactly what you thought to yourself to calm yourself down.

_____

_____

_____

_____

_____

On a scale of 1-100, how anxious were you when you switched to your distraction scene? Score _____

If you're doing it right, your score will go down when you focus on your distraction scene. If your score did go down, say out loud, **"I rule! I own! I can do this!"**

If your scores didn't go down, say to yourself, "I need some more practice at this. It's new to me." Now, take a break and when you come back, try it again just like I described it. Don't be discouraged if it didn't work perfectly the first few times you try it.

If your score did go down and you were able to feel more relaxed, chances are you have just written down a rational or true belief. Look at the belief you just wrote down and ask yourself the following questions:

1) Can I prove the belief to be true?   **Yes No**

2) Is the belief most likely to bring about positive results?   **Yes No**

3) Is the belief likely to get me into or out of trouble?   **into trouble   out of trouble**

Once you've determined the belief is a true/rational belief, **repeat** the same practice exercise **everyday** and **several times a day** if you can. Practice thinking the true/rational belief you've just recorded when you are trying to calm yourself down. Write it down on a small card and carry it with you for times when you feel yourself beginning to get anxious. You can use your distraction scene until you are calmer. Then practice this new, rational thought.

Rational-Emotive Imagery in Action

Here's an example of how REI works in real life. This one is from Jack, who loves to play baseball. He has always been a terrific hitter. This is his first year in a league where kids pitch and it is a whole new ball game. Kids throw the ball all over the place…behind the batter, half-way up the backstop, and a few players get "plunked" or hit with a pitch. At the start of the year, Jack had never been hit but he was very anxious that he might get "plunked" so his hitting was really off. You can't hit if you are backing out of the batter's box.

So after a couple of weeks of Jack ducking and bobbing and weaving around the batter's box, we decided to try to use REI to see if that would help him relax and get back to mashing the ball around the field. I asked Jack what he was saying to himself and he told me, "Some of the pitchers are big and they throw hard and they're wild." We used the same techniques I just described. I had Jack get very relaxed and then he tried to imagine being in the batter's box with a big, hard throwing pitcher on the mound. He closed his eyes and imagined the scene in his mind.

Then I had him imagine the scene but instead of being really anxious, I told him to calm down. I told him to keep imagining the pitcher throwing the ball all over but Jack was suppose to keep working until he could calm himself down.

He wiggled his finger (which is a sign that he was calmer) and I asked him, "What did you say to yourself to calm yourself down?" Jack said, "He'll throw slower so he'll be more accurate and throw strikes."

The final part of REI was to do the SUDS scale. I asked Jack, "In real life when you are up there batting, how anxious are you?" He told me he felt around the 60s or low 70s in real life. I then asked him, "When you are just sitting here imagining the scene, what's your SUDs rating?" He said it dropped down to the 50s when he'd just imagine it. Finally, he said his SUDs rating dropped even further to about 40 when he thought, "He'll throw slower so he'll be more accurate and throw strikes." After that, Jack and I practiced the same REI routine for several days. That was about two weeks ago. Immediately I noticed that Jack was no longer "dancing" around the batter's box so his anxiety had dropped. You could just see that. Pretty soon it was "old Jack" again hitting the ball just like he always used to. Once he had the tools to calm down, his baseball skills could just take over. He's had some up and down games since he started using REI but he'll master his fears because he's got the ideas he can use to help him out. Yes, this "stuff" really does work. I've used it with hundreds of kids over the years and if you try it, commit to it, *and* practice, it **will** help you, too.

One Step at a Time

One of the most common ways to get over a specific anxiety is to start by approaching the problem slowly. You know, taking small steps toward your goal until you are better able to manage the anxiety. Mental health professionals call this systematic desensitization and it is used a lot with kids and adults who have difficulties with anxiety.

If you were afraid of the water, there are a number of ways you could try to conquer your anxiety. You could get in a boat, drive out into the middle of a lake, and jump in. That would be one approach but probably not the best one. You could also start by using a pool. At first, you might need to stand on the deck of the pool and not actually go near the water. After you were able to stand on the deck without being too anxious, maybe you could slowly wade into the water. Maybe you'd have to start the wading in the baby pool. Each day you could go a couple of inches deeper and stay there until you were able to relax. With enough time and plenty of support, you'd eventually be able to go all the way into the water. That's the way systematic desensitization works and we're going to try to help you understand how to apply it to your worries.

One of the first things to do is create a "Fear Thermometer" which is kind of like the SUDs scale. You start by listing the things that you get a little anxious about (like standing on the side of the pool), and you keep going up the thermometer until you list the things you are very anxious about (jumping in the deep end of the pool). The thermometer goes from 1 to 100 so for each event you have to give it a score (or temperature).

Using the pool example, a Fear Thermometer might look like this:

Event	Temperature
Jumping into deep end without life jacket	99
Jumping into deep end with life jacket	90

Wading in chest deep water	75
Wading in waist deep water	65
Wading in knee deep water	50
Walking into the water at a pool	40
Walking into the water at the baby pool	35
Standing on the deck of a pool	20
Looking at a pool	10
Seeing people swimming on video	5

So the plan would be to start at the bottom with video of people swimming. While watching the video, you would repeat a self-calming statement while doing rational-emotive imagery just like we practiced a few pages ago. It might be a self-calming statement like, "I am safe. Nothing bad is going to happen to me in the water" or something like that. Some people use a mental picture of a relaxing event (like clouds floating across the sky) and when they start to feel anxious, they switch to that image. Feel free to experiment to determine which one works best for you. When you can look at that video of someone swimming without feeling overwhelmed by worries, it is time to move to the next event on the Fear Thermometer. You keep using the same set of procedures until you can reach the top of the Fear Thermometer.

Now, it's time for you to make your own Fear Thermometer. I used eight lines but if you need more, feel free to take out a separate sheet of paper.

Event	Temperature

1. _____

_____ Temp._____

2. _____

_____ Temp._____

3. _____

_____ Temp._____

4. _____

_____ Temp._____

5. _____

_____ Temp._____

6. _____

    _____ Temp._____

7. _____

    _____ Temp._____

8. _____

    _____ Temp._____

Write down your self-calming statement or calming mental image you will use to relax here.

_____

_____

_____

_____

_____

    Remember, start at the bottom and when you are able to "manage" that situation without feeling too much anxiety, move up the list. This will take **time** so be patient. Sometimes it will take weeks and even months to work through your list. Don't expect to master the list overnight.

Standing Up To Your Worries

A while back, we examined the way your worries can get out of control. Do you remember this thought bubble?

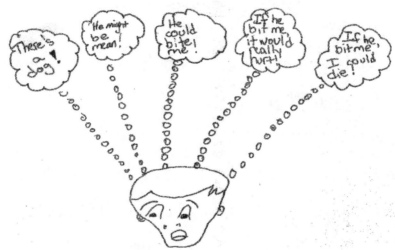

One thing to remember is that your worries are **not** your friends. They seem like they are trying to protect you but they actually make your life more difficult. They make you feel stressed out. In a lot of ways, your worries are like bullies and you know what you have to do with bullies, don't you? **You need to stand up to them**. You need to be tough and talk back

63

to your worries. That's a great way to regain control over your thoughts and feelings. For example, here's a way you could talk back to your worries from above.

1. There's a dog!

1b. Yes, there's a dog. There's a tree. There's the sun. There's nothing to freak out about.

2. He might be mean!

2b. And he might be nice. Look, his tail is wagging. That's a good sign

3. He could bite me!

3b. And he also could lick me or he could chase his tail or do the dog "butt drag" across the lawn.

4. If he bit me, it would really hurt!

4b. It's unlikely that dog will bit me but if he did, it *would* hurt. It probably wouldn't hurt any more than other accidents. I've felt pain hundreds of times before and I can handle it.

5. If he bit me, I might die!

5b. Well, that's really not going to happen. I'm not going to die from a dog bite.

Just like a bully, worries lie to you. Worries tell you everything bad is going to happen and it's not. The worries like to hurt you when you're weak but remember, you're getting stronger each day. Now you've got some ways to fight off the worries.

I've found that some people like to "name" their worries. They come up with a name because once they can name it they seem to have better luck talking back to it. I've had students call their worries the "worry bug." Some have described their worries a "brain hiccup" to show how once they start to worry, it's hard to stop. Take some time and see if you can think of names for your worries then write them down below.

_____

_____

_____

Worry Brain vs. Calm Brain

This activity will give you a chance to practice comparing the different ways of thinking about situations. I call this "Worry Brain vs. Calm Brain." It can be used with any situation you get anxious about but it's a good idea to use it with the one you've been having the most trouble with. Below are two sets of brains. Your job is to write a "Worry Brain" thought and a "Calm Brain" thought in the lines provided.

Let's use the example of being afraid of storms to illustrate what you are supposed to do. In this scenario, you have just seen that the sky is turning dark. The worry brain thinks, "Oh no, it might thunder and lightening and that would be terrible." The calm brain thinks, "Well, there might be a storm but that wouldn't be the worst thing in the world. I'm safe here inside." Next, the worry brain thinks, "It could turn into a tornado and come right at the house." The calm brain thinks, "It could turn into a tornado but it never has before. In fact, in the history of our town, there's never been a single house hit by a tornado. The odds are that I'll be safe." Do you see how it works? This will give your calm brain a chance to practice overpowering your worry brain. Select a situation you get anxious about and practice writing both "Worry Brain" thoughts and then countering that with a "Calm Brain" answers. Give it a shot! Feel free to take out a blank piece of paper and practice this "Worry Brain vs. Calm Brain" all you want. It's easy once you get the hang of it.

1. Worry Brain Though_____

_____

1a. Calm Brain Thought _____

_____

2. Worry Brain Thought _____

_____

2a. Calm Brain Thought _____

_____

Correcting the Worry

Now that you've had some practice telling the difference between worry brain thoughts and calm brain thoughts, it is time to take it one step further. This next activity will give you even more practice changing worries to calming thoughts. Your job is to correct the worry thought. The thoughts below are either totally or partly untrue. I've italicized the key words in each statement to give you a clue as to what makes the belief untrue. Underneath each of these thoughts, correct the worry by writing a new belief. Let's do a couple together. If the worry thought was: "Almost *everything* I worry about actually happens," I could respond by saying, "That's not true. Most of the things I worry about never happen and all my worrying did nothing other than make me feel upset. Sometimes things I worry about happen but 99% of the time they don't."

If the worry thought was, "I *can't take it* when something bad might happen," I could respond by saying, "I **can** take it! I really have no choice but to take it. I cannot control everything that happens but I can control how I react to it." Okay, time for you to take over and do the rest on your own.

1. If I was worrying about something and it did happen, it's usually *10 times worse* than I had imagined.

_____

_____

_____

2. If something bad might happen, I *have to constantly* worry about it.

_____

_____

_____

3. It would be *the worst* if "it" did happen.

_____

_____

_____

4. Because I worry about things, it *proves* I'm *weak and useless*.

_____

_____

_____

Worry Less, Chill More

One of the problems with worries is that they waste a lot of time. You can spend hours each day thinking about your worries and it doesn't accomplish anything. Like we said earlier, worrying about something doesn't keep it from happening! If it did, then worrying might make some sense but worrying has no influence on what is actually going to happen. Thus, worrying = wasted time!

So one of the goals is to cut down on the amount of time you spend worrying. I used to use this idea with students who had anger problems and then it dawned on me that it could be used with kids who worry too much. One way to cut down on the time you spend worrying is to have a specific period of time when it's okay to worry. This should be no longer than 10 minutes and it should be a scheduled for the same time each day. During that time your parents can sit and listen to you talk about your worries or answer questions you may have. This time is your 10 minutes and there shouldn't be other distractions like phone calls.

Let's say you select 2:00-2:10 p.m. for your anxious time. What do you do when a worry pops into your head at 10:00 a.m.? You should try to pop it back out your head until 2:00 p.m. If you try to ask your parents about a worry before 2:00 p.m., they cannot respond to your questions. They can only help you with worries during that special time.

Sometimes it's hard to get that anxiety popped out of your head until 2:00 p.m. Here are a couple of suggestions. Try thinking of your worry like a little person trying to crawl into your ear to get to your brain. When the worry is bugging you, take your hand and pretend to pick it up off your shoulder, put it on the ground and stomp on it! I like that image. You are taking control of your worries by crushing them. Some other students get creative. I knew a student who liked to pretend to pick up the worry, toss it in the air, and then hit it with an imaginary baseball bat or tennis racket. Others make the motion of kicking the worry like a football. Think about the motion you could make to get rid of that worry on your shoulder and draw a picture of it below.

Getting Rid of My Worry! (or "Kicking My Worries to the Curb")

Another suggestion is to pretend to take the worry off your shoulder and put it in your pocket. You can still think about your worry but not right then. It's not the right time. When the time does arrive, go ahead and reach in your pocket and take those worries out and talk them over with your parents.

But you know what happens when that special time of the day gets here? A lot of those worries will be gone. They've left for the day or they just aren't that strong anymore. That's why this idea seems to work. It will allow you to spend less time worrying and it will give you a sense of control over your worries. Give this a try but before you start you'll have to make sure to tell your parents the rules about how this is going to work.

Other Ideas
and Activities

Get Physical

I've often found that when students are stressed out, they worry more. If you learn to manage stress, you'll be in a better position to manage your worries and one of the best ways to fight stress is to exercise. Our country does way too much sitting around so it's time to make an effort to include exercise in your daily routines.

You don't have to be training for a marathon to get positive results from exercise. Working out for as little as thirty minutes a day can have positive results. So right here, right now, let's plan an exercise program.

What type of exercise could you do? Please list three and I'll explain why I want you to list more than one.

1. _____

2. _____

3. _____

What times of the day could you exercise? Remember, a lot of people get up 30 minutes early just to work out.

1. _____

2. _____

3. _____

Here's an important question, what excuses will you use to skip exercising? (You know, "I'm too busy," "Exercising is boring," "I'm too tried." etc.)

1. _____

2. _____

3. _____

Earlier I wanted you to write down at least three different ways you could work out because if you decide you're going to do the same thing everyday, that *will* get boring. It's a good idea to switch it around.

Jack and I would also like to take this opportunity to make few suggestions for ways to keep active.

1) Go for a walk and make yourself a promise that you'll try to start a conversation with at least one person you see on your walk.

2) Go bowling. *Always fun.* Even if you stink and only get a 64, it's still fun.

3) Start a kickball game in your neighborhood. We've come to the conclusion that kickball is the greatest game ever invented (well, it's probably tied with baseball, basketball, and football). No seriously, kickball is massively cool. You really can't have a bad time playing kickball except if you're like me (Jerry) and get the ball stuck in a tree or if everyone kicks line drives off your face. I haven't mastered the art of "ducking" yet.

S-T-O-P

Here's a very simple one that has helped students

I've worked with. Sometimes your worries get into your head and you have a really hard time getting them out.

When this is happening, yell the word "**STOP**" at the top of your lungs. Just yell it out as loud as you can. The S-T-O-P technique helps some people because it's like a shock to their system. I know it seems weird but just try it. You might want to say to your parents, "If I'm in my room and you hear me scream, "STOP", don't worry. I'm just doing something they talked about in the book."

Okay, but what would happen if you were in the middle of a math test and your worries started up? How do you think your teacher and classmates would react to an earth-shattering scream in the middle of the exam? Yeah, they probably wouldn't think it's too funny so here's what you do. Write the word "STOP" on an index card and keep it with you. If you get stuck in a place where you can't yell the word, take the card out of your pocket and *scream it in your mind*. Just imagine screaming the word but don't actually make a sound.

The Rubber Band Technique

This is very similar to the S-T-O-P technique we just described but instead of screaming a word when the worries get stuck in your brain, you are to snap your wrist with a rubber band. Just wear a rubber band around your wrist and when you can't shake the worries, pull the rubber band back and give yourself a little "snap." Sometimes this helps to break the thought cycle.

Celebrate Success

When you are able to overcome your worries and face a scary situation, you should celebrate that success. By celebrate that success I don't necessarily mean throw yourself a "blow out party" but that might be okay, too! Use your success to build your confidence by reminding yourself that you can "do it."

Last summer our family was in Canada and had a chance to go up into the tallest building in the world; the CN Tower in Toronto. Jack wasn't thrilled about the idea but we all encouraged him and reassured him it was safe. Well, after he worried in the line for forty minutes we got in the elevator and rode up over 1,800 feet! I think I can speak for everyone in my family when I say it was awesome. Jack had the most fun of all and he even went out onto the glass floor (something his sister, Anna, wouldn't do). Since that time we've used the CN Tower to remind him that if he had let his worries bully him around he would have missed out on a great experience.

Assume the Worst

One of the things Jack and I did to help him learn to manage his worries was to ask a very simple question: "What's the worst thing that could happen?"

Here we are, standing on a glass floor, 1800 feet off the ground!

When Jack was totally spazzed out about getting hit by the baseball I asked him that question. Our conversation went like this:

Jerry: So what's the worst thing that could happen?

Jack: I could get hit by the baseball.

Jerry: Yep, you sure could. What would happen then?

Jack: It would really hurt.

Jerry: It would hurt. It hurts to get plunked. How long do you think it would hurt?

Jack: I don't know.

Jerry: Remember in the last game Hunter got hit. He went to first base. Did you see him rubbing his leg?

Jack: No.

Jerry: Did you see him running the bases? Was he running slower than usual?

Jack: No. He ran okay.

Jerry: So how long do you think it hurt?

Jack: Not very long.

Jerry: You've gotten hit by the ball plenty of times already. You've had groundballs hit you on the arms and legs. Those hurt I know but you've been okay after a little while. Those balls being pitched to you aren't really going any faster than a hard groundball.

Sometimes when you talk about "the worst thing" you quickly realize that the worst thing isn't really that bad. Once again, it's your mind making a mountain out of a molehill. Kids who worry too much are usually good at making mountains out of molehills.

Think of one of your # 1 worry and write it down below.

_____

_____

Now, if this did happen, why would it be so terrible? If it did happen, would it totally destroy all the "good stuff" in life? **Yes No**
Would it stop the production of ice cream? **Yes No**
If your worry did happen, would your favorite T.V. show immediately go off the air? **Yes No**
Would you go to school 365 days a year? **Yes No**

Like I've said before, when the event does take place, it's usually "no fun" but we survive it. The worrying about the event is often worse than the event itself.

About 15 years ago, my kidneys stopped working. As you probably know, people need kidneys to clean their blood and filter fluid out of their bodies. We can't live without kidneys. Not long after that I was diagnosed with a very serious liver disease (lucky me!). Obviously, this was a time filled with worries for my family. I went about three days without sleeping because I was so freaked out! After a few months I had to go on something called dialysis, which is a process used to artificially clean my blood. It involved a lot of big needles and weird looking machines. During that time my life could have been described as "less than awesome."

I finally got sick and tired of being worried all the time so I asked myself the very same question I asked you: What's the worst thing that could happen? The answer was obvious. I could die.

Once I finally accepted the fact that I was very sick and could quite possible die from these diseases, I started to feel calmer. I know that sounds strange but it's true. Once I faced up to the fact that I might not survive, I was able to get a better handle on my situation. I was sick and tired of all the worrying. I was not going to be ruled by my worries. There were lots of things that stunk about my situation but I could still do some of my favorite activities. I could still rock out and shred on my guitar. I was still married to a beautiful, intelligent, funny, and supportive wife. Even though I was very sick, I could see people all around me who were worse off than I was so I decided that I was through being controlled by my worries.

Fast forward 15 years and I'm happy to tell you that I received a kidney transplant and I'm doing great. Sure, I have to take a bunch of pills, but big deal. My health problems taught me amazing lessons that I never could have learned otherwise.

Now it's time to measure how much you've changed since the start of this book. Once again, complete the anxiety survey below as honestly as possible. There are no right or wrong answers, just circle the number which best reflects how strongly you agree or disagree with each statement. When you've finished, compare this score with your score earlier in the book. If you're less anxious, your score will go **down**. If you've actually done worse with your anxiety, your score will go **up**.

The Anxiety Survey

Strongly   Strongly

Disagree   Agree

1. If something bad might happen, I have to worry about it.

   1   2   3   4   5   6

2. I have no control over my worrying.

   1   2   3   4   5   6

3. Worrying about something can keep it from happening.

     1   2   3   4   5   6

4. If what I worry about *did* happen, it would be the worst thing in the world.

     1   2   3   4   5   6

5. Worries have a "mind of their own" and can't be managed.

     1   2   3   4   5   6

6. If what I worry about *did* happen, I couldn't stand it.

     1   2   3   4   5   6

7. Because I worry about things, it proves I'm worthless and weak.

     1   2   3   4   5   6

8. Worries never seem to go away. Once you've got them, you're stuck with them.

     1   2   3   4   5   6

TOTAL from the first Anxiety Survey _____

Decreased by _____ Say, "I'm doing better!"

Increased by _____ Say, "I need to keep working!"

Summary

I've used these exercises and practice activities with hundreds of students over the years and I can predict where most of you will be at the finish.

1) **Some of you will have made great progress.**

You will already be well on your way to controlling your worries instead of letting your worries control you. You've worked hard at the lessons and really practiced. **You** are in charge of your thoughts, reactions, and feelings.

2) **Some of you will be making progress but still struggling.**

You'll understand that your thoughts largely create your anxiety but haven't learned how to keep yourself from getting anxious. Another way of saying this is, "You can talk the talk, but not walk the walk." You understand it, but cannot live it yet.

That's okay. Learning these skills is not easy.

You've had a habit of getting worried for a long time and it takes hard work to overcome this tendency. Focus on the distraction technique, which was explained in an earlier chapter, until you do become better at arguing yourself out of your anxiety.

3) **Some will feel it is hopeless.**

You might even believe that there is now way to ever overcome your problems with worries. **Not True.** It just takes more work. Think about it this way for a minute.

Whenever you're learning something totally new, there is a time when you can't do it and this new skill seems hopeless. There were times when you were younger when you used to be anxious about certain things but you've learned to manage those feelings now that you're older. For example, when I was little I used to be afraid of dentists. I'm not anymore. Jack used to afraid of getting "plunked" by the baseball. He's not anymore. Below, write down something you used to be afraid of but aren't anymore.

The very fact that you have mastered one set of worries is *proof* that you *can* learn how to do this so…**Don't give up**! Don't hand over control of your life to your worries. Don't let the worries win. Keep trying, keep working, and keep *believing* that you can do it because you can.